Why are Mexicans buying up all the Cabbage Patch Dolls?
(see page 10)

What's black, charred, and hangs from a chandelier?
(see page 16)

Did you hear about Ben Hur's sex-change operation?
(see page 70)

What's another name for AIDS?
(see page 74)

What do you get when you screw a leper?
(see page 89)

What's the definition of alimony?
(see page 97)

Also by Blanche Knott
Available from St. Martin's Press

Truly Tasteless Jokes IV

Truly Tasteless Jokes V

Blanche Knott's

Truly Tasteless Jokes VI

St. Martin's Press
New York

ST. MARTIN'S PRESS TITLES ARE AVAILABLE AT
QUANTITY DISCOUNTS FOR SALES PROMOTIONS,
PREMIUMS OR FUND RAISING. SPECIAL BOOKS
OR BOOK EXCERPTS CAN ALSO BE CREATED TO
FIT SPECIFIC NEEDS. FOR INFORMATION WRITE
TO SPECIAL SALES MANAGER, ST. MARTIN'S
PRESS, 175 FIFTH AVENUE, NEW YORK, N.Y. 10010.

BLANCHE KNOTT'S TRULY TASTELESS JOKES VI
Copyright © 1986 by Blanche Knott

ISBN: 0-312-90361-8
Can. ISBN: 0-312-90373-1

St. Martin's Press
175 Fifth Avenue
New York, New York 10010

for Clyde

CONTENTS

Truly
Tasteless
Jokes
VI

ETHNIC VARIEGATED

Did you hear about the psychic Puerto Rican who knew the exact day and minute he would die?

The warden told him.

•

Three minority crews were competing for a contract with the telephone company. In order to select the most qualified, the phone company instructed each crew to go out and see how many telephone poles it could erect in one day. At the end of the day the Jewish crew reported thirty-five poles to the impressed phone company official. "Good, but not good enough," he told the Italians, who had installed thirty-two. "Well?" he asked, turning to the Polish crew.

"Two," said the foreman proudly.

"So why are you so proud of yourself? Those guys did thirty-five," pointed out the phone guy.

"Yeah," said the Polish foreman, "but look how much they left sticking out of the ground."

•

What's the difference between a black and a Pakistani?
  Five more minutes in the oven.

.

Why's a car engine like an Italian girl?
  On a cold morning when you really need it, it won't turn over.

.

There was once a mobster who employed a deaf-and-dumb accountant. He was satisfied with the guy's work until the year he decided to double-check the books and found that he was short two million dollars, so he sent out a couple of goons to bring the guy into his office. An hour or so later the cowering accountant arrived, accompanied by his brother, who could speak sign language. "You tell that son of a bitch I want to know where my two million bucks is at," boomed the mobster.

  After a quick exchange with his brother, the translator reported that the accountant knew nothing about it.

  The boss stood up, pulled out a gun, and came around the desk to hold it against the accountant's neck. "You tell this son of a bitch that if he doesn't tell me where the dough is, I'm going to blow his brains out—*after* I have the boys work him over."

  This was duly translated to the quaking accountant, who gestured frantically to his brother, explaining that the money was stashed in three shoe boxes in his closet.

  "So whaddid he say?" interrupted the gangster impatiently.

  The translator turned and replied, "He says you haven't got the balls."

.

Why were two Mexicans on "That's Incredible"?
  One had car insurance and the other was an only child.

.

Did you hear about the Italian who was asked to become a Jehovah's Witness?

He refused because he hadn't seen the accident.

•

Out for an expedition in the country, an American, a German, and a Pole realized that night was falling and they needed somewhere to spend the night. After a long walk, they came to a farm and asked if they could sleep in the barn. The farmer gave his permission and sent the American up to the top of the hayloft, the German to the middle level, and the Pole to a pile of hay on the ground floor.

Late that night the American felt the urge to take a crap, and since there was no toilet in the barn he did his business in his pillowcase and tossed it over the side of the hayloft. Soon after, the German encountered the same problem and solved it in the same way.

The next morning the farmer offered breakfast to the travelers and asked how they had slept. "Just fine, thanks," said the American.

"Very well," answered the German.

"Not too bad," replied the Pole, "but I had to beat the shit out of two ghosts."

•

What do you call a Syrian shepherd driving fifty ewes towards a PLO base?

A pimp.

•

Chinese VD?

Ping-Pong balls.

•

Why did the Russian sew fur in his shorts?

He wanted ball-to-ball carpeting.

•

Can you figure out this Italian wedding invitation?
    You, 2A wedding Rosa Mister.
    (Read it aloud, punctuation included.)

•

A tourist visiting Mexico for the first time got off the train at
a hot, dusty little town. Immediately wondering when the
next train out would be along, he went over and asked the
time of a scroungy old man who was leaning against a wall
next to his donkey.
    The old guy appeared to fondle his donkey's balls, then
answered, "It's five minutes after eleven."
    "That's amazing!" said the tourist. "How do you do it?"
    "Not much to it," explained the Mexican. "There's a
clock on the wall over there and my donkey's balls are in the
way."

•

What should you do if you have bulemia?
    Propose to an Ethiopian.

•

How do you know when an Ethiopian is pregnant?
    You can see the baby.

•

What's this?

An Ethiopian family portrait.

•

One weekend Jerzy and Luigi went hunting. Coming to a clearing by the side of a lake, they caught sight of a beautiful blonde girl sunning herself on the rocks in the nude. "Mama mia," gasped Luigi as she stood up and headed for the water's edge, "that woman's so beautiful I could eat her!"

So Jerzy shot her.

•

A sailor from the Greek Navy was stranded on a desert island and managed to survive by making friends with the natives—such good friends, in fact, that one day the chief offered him his daughter for the evening. That night, while he was banging away at her, the chief's daughter kept shouting, "Aguma! Aguma!" which the sailor figured is what the natives say when they think something is really great.

A few days later the chief invited the sailor to play golf, and hit a hole-in-one. Anxious to try out his new vocabulary, the sailor enthusiastically shouted, "Aguma!"

The chief turned around with a perplexed expression and asked, "What do you mean, 'wrong hole'?"

•

How does a WASP start his new car?
  With a key.

•

Hear about the disadvantaged WASP?
  He grew up with a black-and-white TV.

•

Paddy O'Casey was on his deathbed when his wife, Colleen, tiptoed into the bedroom and asked if he had any last requests.

"Actually, my dear, there is one thing I really would like before I go off to that great shamrock patch in the sky,"

Paddy whispered. "A piece of that wonderful chocolate cake of yours."

"Ah, me darlin', have a patata instead," his wife exclaimed. "I'm saving the cake for the wake."

•

What do you call a group of Mexicans holding hands around a house?
  A spicket fence.

•

Did you hear about the Mexican who was killed in a pie-eating contest?
  A cow stepped on his head.

•

What's an Ethiopian with feathers up his ass?
  A dart.

•

Why is the Ethiopian school day so short?
  They skip lunch.

•

What do you call an Ethiopian in a fur coat?
  A pipe cleaner.

•

How many Ethiopians does it take to change a light bulb?
  None. They can't afford them.

•

"Lookit my new watch," said one Aggie to another. "This here shows what time it is now. And when you push this little button, you can see what time it was at this exact time yesterday."

•

First guy: "Hey, those are nice shoes. What kind are they?"
   Second guy: "They're Italian shoes."
   First guy: "Italian shoes?"
   Second guy: "Yeah. Wherever I go, dago!"

•

What do Laotians call the dogcatcher's truck?
   Meals on wheels.

•

What's a Laotian's favorite meal?
   Mutt loaf.

•

When the son of a wealthy Italian industrialist was kidnapped, his parents waited impatiently for word from his abductors. The first contact was a box which arrived on the doorstep containing the boy's left ear.
   "Magnifico!" exclaimed the magnate. "As soon as we get alla his parts, we can putta him back together again."

•

How do you clear out a K Mart?
   Yell, "Immigration!"

•

What do Mexicans call K-Mart shopping carts?
  Baby buggies.

•

Teacher's instructions in an integrated high school:
  TWO PLUS DOS EQUALS FOE.

•

Hear about the Aggie who was majoring in animal husbandry?
  They caught him at it.

•

Why are there no more Catholics in Mexico City?
  They're all Quakers.

•

What's the name of the Mexican version of "Roots"?
  "Joints."

•

One day Barbara Walters was doing a special on the customs of the American Indians. After touring a reservation, she asked her guide about the difference in the number of feathers in various men's headdresses.

  "Me only have one feather because me only have one squaw," was the brave's explanation.

  Thinking this was a joke, Ms. Walters put the question to another brave, who said, "Ugh. Me only have four feathers because only have four squaws."

  Somewhat perturbed, Ms. Walters decided to interview the chief. "Why are there so many feathers in your headdress?" she asked.

  "Me chief, so me fuck 'em all—big, small, short, tall, me fuck 'em all."

Ms. Walters was horrified. "You ought to be hung!"

"You damn right," said the chief, "me hung like buffalo."

Ms. Walters cried, "You don't have to be so damn hostile!"

"Hoss-style, dog-style, wolf-style, any style. Me fuck 'em all."

Tears in her eyes, Ms. Walters cried, "Oh, dear . . ."

"No deer," said the chief. "Asshole too high and fuckers run too fast. Me no fuck deer."

•

How can you tell Italian women are embarrassed by their long black hair?

Because they wear long black gloves to cover it up.

•

What's this? (Hold up a comb.)

One hundred Ethiopians carrying a canoe.

•

I don't see what's the big deal about an Ethiopian walking twenty miles for food rations—some diabetics would give an arm or a leg just for a cookie.

•

What are the three words a Greek prostitute hears most often?

"Turn over, honey."

•

How can you tell a Jamaican prostitute?

Pubic dreadlocks.

•

What do you say to a Mexican business executive?
  "I'll take a nickel bag."

•

What's the Haitian national anthem?
  "Row, row, row your boat . . ."

•

How about the national anthem of Ethiopia?
  "Aren't you hungry . . ."

•

Italian woman: "Oh, Gino, you are the world's greatest lover!"
  French woman: "Ah, Jacques, you are marvelous. More, more!"
  Jewish woman: "Oy, Jake, the ceiling needs painting."

•

Why are Mexicans buying up all the Cabbage Patch dolls?
  To get birth certificates.

•

A soldier in Vietnam walked into a whorehouse in Saigon, went up to the madam, and asked, "Do Oriental women really have horizontal cunts?"
  "Why?" asked the madam. "Are you harmonica player?"

•

Why do Mexicans eat their young?
  Because there'll always be enough to go around.

•

Mr. Weinberg came home unexpectedly and found his wife in bed with another man. Furious, he cried, "What are you doing?"

"See," said Mrs. Weinberg, turning to her lover, "I told you he was stupid."

•

What do you get when you cross an Irishman and a Jew?
    An alcoholic who buys his liquor wholesale.

•

What did the South African girl give her boyfriend?
    Apart-head.

•

What do you call a Nicaraguan birth-control pill?
    A CONTRA-ceptive.

•

Why do Chinese people have slanted eyes?
    (Put your palms to your temples and pull back.) "Oh, no—not rice again!"

•

Three men in an airplane crash, die, and go to hell. They happen to catch the Devil in a good mood, and he tells them that for twenty dollars apiece they could return to earth alive. After the offer was discussed for a bit, the Irishman pulled out twenty dollars and—POOF!—found himself back at home.

"What the hell happened to you?" asked his wife. After he explained, she asked curiously, "So where are the other two?"

"Got me," said the Irishman. "When I left, the Jew had the Devil down to seventeen-fifty and the black said he should be getting a check from the government any day now."

POLISH

HOW DO YOU KEEP A POLISH MAN BUSY?

(over)

HOW DO YOU KEEP A POLISH MAN BUSY?

(over)

Hear about the famous Polish doctor?
He performed the first successful hemorrhoid transplant.

·

Three Poles were locked out of their car and didn't know
what to do.

The first said, "I know, let's bend a coat hanger. We'll
snake it between the driver's side window and the car's
frame and try to lift the button up."

"No way," countered the second Pole, "that'll take too
much time. We should use a crowbar and pry the door
open."

"I don't care what you guys use," spoke up the third fellow. "I just wish you'd hurry up and decide, because it looks
like it's going to rain and the top's down."

·

What wears green slacks, a red shirt, a purple polka-dot tie,
a straw hat, and sits on a wall?
Humpty Dumptski.

·

A Pole walked into a saloon and saw a gorilla sitting at the
bar drinking a beer. "That's a pretty strange sight," he commented to the bartender.

"You think that's strange, watch this," the bartender replied. Reaching under the bar for a baseball bat, he walked
up behind the animal and hit him on the head as hard as he
could. The gorilla fell to the floor and the bartender went
back behind the bar. Thirty seconds later, the gorilla got up,
walked over to the bartender, and gave him a blow job.

"You want to give it a try?" the bartender asked after the
gorilla had returned to his beer.

"Hell no," said the Pole in amazement. "I don't think I
could get up off the floor!"

·

Why do Poles spray-paint their trash cans orange?

So their children will think they're eating at Howard Johnson's.

•

Pole: "I want a coat for my wife."
  Furrier: "Mink?"
  Pole: "She's got one."
  Furrier: "Sable?"
  Pole: "She's got one."
  Furrier: "Skunk?"
  Pole: "Skunk!"
  Furrier: "Why not? It's just a pussy that smells bad."
  Pole: "Oh, she's got one of those too."

•

What's black, charred, and hangs from a chandelier?
  A Polish electrician.

•

Did you hear about the Pole who couldn't count to twenty-one unless he was naked?

•

Stanley was an avid golfer. Even though he spent almost all his spare time on the links, he managed to meet a woman, and after a while he decided she was really the one for him. "I want you to marry me, Laura," he said earnestly, "but there's something I want you to know first. . . ."

Laura blushed, because she had never told Stanley that before meeting him she had earned her living as a prostitute.

"I love golf," Stanley went on. "In fact I live for golf, and I want you to understand that it's going to take up a lot of my time."

"I don't mind in the least, dear," said Laura. "In fact I

have something of a confession for you too. You see, I used to be a hooker."

"No problem, honey. Just open your right hand. . . ."

•

Did you hear about the Pole who put Odor-Eaters in his shoes, walked three steps, and disappeared?

•

Trying to light his cigarette, a Polish man struck a match. It didn't ignite, so he threw it away and struck a second one. No luck there, so he threw it away too and tried a third match. When it lit, he blew it out and said, "That's a good one—I've got to save it."

•

Why did the Polish hippie take two hits of LSD?
    He wanted to go on a round trip.

•

Polish want ad:
        BE A GARBAGE COLLECTOR
    $500 A WEEK AND ALL YOU CAN EAT!

•

First Pole: "Have you ever read Shakespeare?"
    Second Pole: "No, who wrote it?"

•

Did you hear about the little Polish kid who wouldn't ride on the roller coaster because he didn't have a return ticket?

•

How about the Polish mother who kept an ice pack on her breast to keep the milk fresh?

•

Okay, how about the Pole who phoned a camera store and asked if they rented flashbulbs?

•

A Pole was driving along a country road when he spied an unusual sight. Off to the side, a farmer was pulling frantically at a calf's leg protruding from a pregnant cow. Seeing that the farmer could use some help, the Pole stopped his car and ran over, grabbed on to the calf's other leg, and yanked with all his might.

Finally, after much struggling, they managed safely to extract the baby cow. "Thank you kindly, neighbor," said the farmer, wiping the sweat off his forehead. "How much do I owe you for your help?"

"You don't owe me a thing, but please answer one question," responded the Pole. "Just how fast was the calf running when it hit that cow's ass?"

•

Why did the Pole unwind his toilet paper?
  To find out where he left off.

•

Two Poles were walking down the street. "Hey," said one to the other, "look at that dead bird!"

His friend looked up in the sky and asked, "Where?"

•

How does a Pole keep his dinner warm?
  He puts tinfoil up his nose.

•

Then there were the two Poles speeding down the highway at one hundred miles per hour. "Hey," asked the driver, "see any cops following us?"

"Yup."

"Shit. Are his flashers on?"

His passenger turned back, thought it over, and answered, "Yup . . . nope . . . yup . . . nope . . . yup . . ."

•

Hear about the Pole who bought a Trans-Am?

It took him a month to realize he could drive it at night.

•

How can you spot a level-headed Pole?

He drools from both sides of his mouth.

•

How do you know Batman's Polish?

He wears his jockey shorts over his leotards.

•

Two Polish carpenters were putting siding on a house when one looked over at the other and asked, "Why the hell are you throwing away those nails?"

"Oh," replied the second Pole, "these nails have the heads on the wrong end."

"You dummy," the first Pole yelled, "those are for the other side of the house!"

•

What's a Polish birth certificate?

A refund from the Trojan rubber company.

•

Police Captain: "He got away, did he? Didn't I tell you to cover all of the exits?"

Polish cop: "Yes, sir, I did, sir. But he must have left through one of the entrances."

•

I once knew a Pole who tried to write "Happy Birthday" on a cake, but he ruined it getting it into the typewriter.

•

Two Poles went deer hunting and managed to shoot a big buck. Each grabbed a hind leg, and they were pulling it through the woods when they happened across a game warden. After making sure their hunting licenses were in order, the warden said, "If you don't mind a suggestion, fellas, you'll have an easier time pulling that deer along if you hold it by the antlers instead of the feet."

The Poles decided he probably knew what he was talking about, so they each took hold of an antler and started off again. "He was right," commented one a few minutes later. "This really is easier."

"Yeah," said his buddy, "but we're getting farther from the truck."

•

How can you tell a Pole with weak kidneys?

Rusty zipper and yellow socks.

JEWISH

At the conclusion of the physical exam, the doctor summoned his patient into his office with a very grave look on his face. "I hate to be the one to break it to you, Fred," he said, "but I'm afraid you've got cancer. An advanced case too—you've only got six months to live."

"Oh, my God," gasped Fred, turning white. When the news had sunk in, he said, "Listen, Doc, you've known me a long time. Do you have any suggestions as to how I could make the most of my remaining months?"

"Have you ever married?" asked the doctor.

Fred explained that he'd been a bachelor all his life.

"You might think about taking a wife," the doctor proposed. "After all, you'll need someone to look after you during the final illness."

"That's a good point, Doc," mused Fred. "And with only six months to live I'd better make the most of my time."

"May I make one more suggestion?" asked the doctor. When Fred nodded, he said, "Marry a Jewish girl."

"A Jewish girl—how come?" wondered Fred.

"It'll seem longer."

•

What's the difference between a JAP and a freezer?
  You have to plug in a freezer.

•

What's a Jewish ménage à trois?
  Using both hands to masturbate.

•

How's Christmas celebrated in a Jewish home?
  They put parking meters on the roof.

•

Why did the Jewish mother have herself entombed at
Bloomingdale's?
  So her daughter would visit at least twice a week.

•

Heard the difference between a JAP and a toilet?
  After you use it, the toilet doesn't follow you around for
six months, whining.

•

Reuben and Meyer were both gin rummy addicts. One day
they met in the card room at the country club, and it just
happened to be the day after Reuben's wife had been discovered in bed with Meyer.
  "Look," said Reuben, "I know you've been screwing my
wife, but I still love her, so let's settle this in a civilized way.
We'll play a game of gin and the winner gets to keep her."
  "Okay," agreed Meyer, "but just to make it interesting,
let's play for a penny a point."

•

What do you call ten JAPs in the basement?
  A whine cellar.

•

Did you hear about the JAP sorority?
  Sigma Theta, Nu?

•

What does a black Jew say?
  "Gimme five . . . percent!"

•

What does a JAP say when she's reaching orgasm?
  "Mom, I've got to hang up now. . . ."

•

Did you hear about the new Jewish bank?
  When you call up, the teller complains, "You never visit. You never write. You only call when you want money."

•

BLACK

Why are black men hung better than white men?
   Because little white boys had *toys* to play with.

•

What makes blacks so horny?
   Afro-disiacs.

•

What do a pimp and a farmer have in common?
   They both need a hoe to stay in business.

•

A white man walks into a bar wearing a button that says, "I hate niggers," and sits down at the bar.
   "Listen, buddy, some people here won't appreciate that button. You'd better take it off," the bartender warns.
   "I don't care," says the man. "I hate niggers. They're dumb, stupid, and smelly. I just hate 'em."

Shaking his head, the bartender goes to serve another customer. Five minutes later a big black man walks in and sits down next to the man with the button.

"Hey," the black man says, spying the button for the first time, "I don't like that. Take it off or I'll take it off for you."

"Hell no," replies the white man, "I hate niggers. They're dumb and stupid. I hate them."

"Then I'll just have to remove it for you," counters the black man. "Let's go outside."

Both men go out to the alley behind the bar, and the black whips out a huge switchblade.

"See, *see* how stupid you niggers are," the white man chuckles, "bringing a knife to a gunfight."

•

Why do blacks keep their fists closed when making the black-power sign?

If they held out an open palm, they'd fall out of the trees.

•

What's the African mating call?

"Here I is!"

•

What do you call sex with a black man?

Rape.

•

Hear about the black woman who was filling out a job application?

When she got to the question about "sex," she checked both "M" and "F" and wrote in "sometimes on Wednesdays too."

•

Two flies were having a race across a black man's lips. After each had won one race, they decided to run a tie breaker. Panting, the one fly reached the finish line, only to discover his friend had already arrived with time to spare.

"How did you do that?" he inquired.

"Oh, it was easy," his friend explained. "I took a shortcut around his head."

•

Why do black men like pussy so much?

Because the inside looks like watermelon and the outside smells like catfish.

•

Why don't blacks take aspirin?

They're too proud to pick the cotton out of the bottle.

•

An excited black woman calls her husband at work to give him some good news about their son, Leroy.

"Honey," she squeals, "Leroy done said his first half word!"

"His first half word?" repeated the father.

"Yeah, he done said 'Mother'!"

•

What do you call a black with no arms?

Trustworthy.

•

Know why carmakers in Detroit aren't putting seat belts into any automobiles purchased by blacks?

They felt it would be safer to put Velcro on the headrests.

•

Why does the Hartz Mountain Tick and Flea Collar come in fluorescent colors?

So blacks can wear costume jewelry too.

•

Did you hear why the Ku Klux Klan purchased the movie rights to "Roots"?

They want to show it backwards so it has a happy ending.

•

A black couple was driving through the countryside in an old, beat-up Volkswagen. The fertile quiet of the scenery began to inspire some lascivious thoughts, so they decided to pull over to the side of the road and fuck. The girl quickly jumped out of the cramped car, stripped, lay spread-eagled on the lush, green grass, and waited. And waited. And waited.

"Honey," she yelled, "if yo' don' get out of dat Volkswagen, I's won't be in the mood much longer!"

"Baby," he lamented, "if I don' get out of the mood, I won' get out of this here Volkswagen!"

•

What do you call a white woman who dates a black man?

Color blind.

•

Why do black women have such big purses?

To carry their lipstick.

•

A schoolteacher announced to her third-grade class that the subject for the day was farm animals.

"Can anybody tell me what sound a chicken makes?" she asked.

"Cluck, cluck, cluck," Tommy answered proudly.

"That's correct, Tommy," the teacher said. "Does anyone know what a cow says?"

Sally's hand shot up as she yelled, "Moooo!"

"Very good, Sally. Now, who knows what a pig sounds like?" she queried.

From the back of the room, little Rasmus shouted, "FREEZE, MUTHERFUCKER!"

•

What's a black mermaid?
    A carp with tits.

•

Why shouldn't you run over a black on a bike?
    It might be your bike.

•

In school one day, a black kid walks up to his white classmate and says, "My dad has a new car, and the horn goes 'Honkey, Honkey.'"

The white kid laughs and responds, "That's nothing, my pop just got a new chain saw and when he pulls the cord, it goes, 'Runnigger, Runnigger.'"

•

Who were the three most famous women in black history?
    Aunt Jemima, Diana Ross, and Mother Fucker.

•

What does a black man use for a condom?
    A duffel bag.

•

Did you hear that President Reagan appointed a black man as an ambassador . . . to the Bermuda Triangle?

•

A little black kid went to the market to buy a wheel of cheese. Returning from the market, the boy dropped the cheese and it rolled down the street, where it came to rest at the feet of a white guy. He picked it up and brought it home to his wife. "What kind of cheese is that?" she asked after he showed her what he had found.

"I guess it's nacho cheese," the husband replied.

"How do you know that?" she inquired.

"Well," the man said, "this little black boy kept following me and yelling something like, 'It's nach yo' cheese, it's nach yo' cheese!'"

•

What's black and white and red all over?

A Ku Klux Klan house-warming party.

•

What did the little black kid say when Santa came down the chimney saying, "Ho, ho, ho?"

"Where's my mama, motherfucker?"

•

Hear about the black mom who named her children Syphilis and Gonorrhea?

She found those pretty names on the birth certificates.

•

This black man was down on his luck, sitting on a curb in skid row slugging the last of his Thunderbird, when an angel appeared next to him. Saying how sorry she felt for him, she asked about his life and found out Sam had been a window washer, and a pretty good window washer at that.

"Well, why don't you go to L.A.," suggested the angel, "and see if you can't land a job window-washing on some of those skyscrapers out there?"

This struck Sam as a pretty good idea, so he cleaned up his act, hitched a ride to California, landed a job, and was doing fine when one day the angel materialized on the thirty-ninth-floor window ledge right next to him. "So do you believe in angels now?" she asked sweetly.

"I sure do," answered the window washer.

"And would you put all your trust in God?"

"You bet," said Sam.

"And if you undid your harness and leaned back off the ledge, do you think God would hold you safe?" asked the angel. Sam nodded confidently, undid his harness, and fell thirty-nine stories—SPLAT!—to the sidewalk.

The little angel shook her head, looked up at the sky, and murmured, "Lord, I just don't see how I ever made it into heaven, hating black folks the way I do. . . ."

•

Two black men from Seattle head up to Vancouver for the weekend in their white Eldorado. On arrival they check into a motel, purchase a quart of Ripple, and proceed to sip and sightsee until they're feeling very good indeed. Noticing an auction in progress, they decide to go in and have some fun making ridiculous bids, and all goes well until they bid one dollar for a gorilla. There's dead silence as the auctioneer intones, "Going, going, *gone!*"

Having no choice, the two guys lead the gorilla back to their motel on a leash, sit him on one of the beds, and try and figure out what to do. "Hey, man," says Titus, "how we gonna get this beast 'cross the border?"

Lemoyne thinks and thinks. "Shoot, man," he says, "let's just dump him in the back seat and go for it." But the border guards turn them back, and the next night finds them sitting in the same motel room until Titus comes up with a plan. Driving by Goodwill, they pick up a long-sleeved dress, lipstick, and some flashy earrings. Dressing the ape in this finery, they put him between the two of them and head for the border.

After looking them over carefully, the guard waves them through, then turns to his fellow guard with a disgusted look. "Joe," he says, "why is it that every time you see a good-looking Polish girl, she's with two black guys?"

•

What did God say when he made the first black?
  "Oh, shit!"

•

A Halloween party was being held at the neighborhood school and this little black kid wanted to go so bad that he immediately started looking for a costume. Dressing up in a black suit and top hat, he went into the kitchen and asked, "Mom, who is I?"

"Son, who is you?" she had to ask.

"I'se Abraham Lincoln."

"You can't be," she said. "He was twice as tall as you, and he was white."

The kid went back upstairs, draped himself in a sheet, and came back downstairs, where he had to explain to his mother that he was dressing up as Gandhi. "You can't be," she said. "Gandhi was bald, and he liberated India from the British Empire. You're supposed to be stupid, but don't abuse the privilege."

So the little boy went back upstairs, took off all his clothes, and shoved a two-by-four up his ass. "Mom, who is I?" he asked.

"Son, who is you?" she replied.

"I'se a Fudgsicle."

•

Fred "Big Boy" Jones came into a bar and proclaimed, "I'm the biggest, baddest player in the NFL. I make $250,000 a year, I drive a Mercedes-Benz, and I only fuck white women. Now who wants to buy me a drink?" An offer promptly came from a guy sitting at the bar. After he'd downed it, Jones announced, "I'm the biggest, baddest player in the NFL, I make $250,000 a year, I drive a Mercedes-Benz, and I only fuck white women. Who wants to buy me a drink?" Another guy spoke up, and after they'd shared a whiskey and some conversation, Jones made his speech again.

A third man waved the football player over, but after only a few seconds Jones hauled back, punched the guy so hard he passed out cold, and stomped out of the bar. When the guy came to, his friends were gathered around him, dying to know what had happened. "All I said," he explained, shaking his head in bewilderment, "was that if I made $250,000 a year, I wouldn't fuck niggers either."

•

Finding out that Alabama was starting up a hunting season on blacks, a young redneck rushed to obtain a license and stock up on shells. Soon he was riding down a country road where he came across a whole bunch of blacks picking watermelons in a field. Screeching to a halt, he opened fire, only to be promptly accosted by a game warden who shouted, "What the hell do you think you're doing?"

"I got a license right here," protested the sportsman.

"Maybe so," countered the official, "but not to hunt in a baited field."

HANDICAPPED

Did you hear about the new Helen Keller disease?
  It's called the clap.

•

Why do you tie a baby's umbilical cord?
  If you don't, he goes wwhhoooooosssssshhhhh!

•

Why did the man like having a midget for a girlfriend?
  Because she always wanted to go up on him.

•

How do you find a blind man in a nudist colony?
  It ain't hard.

•

Why did Helen Keller marry a black man?
  It was easy to read his lips.

.

What's the definition of chaos?
  A busload of Jerry's kids passing a magnet factory.

.

What's red and silver and walks into walls?
  A baby with forks in its eyes.

.

What's charred black, and screams?
  A baby getting his toy out of the fireplace.

.

What smells bad and screams?
  A baby chewing on a lamp cord.

.

How did the dead baby cross the road?
  It got stuck in someone's exhaust pipe.

.

What's red and white and bobs up and down?
  A baby in a Jacuzzi.

.

What's red and black and jumps in the air?
  Same baby in a toaster.

.

Two babies in a crib:
  Girl baby: "Rape! Rape!"
  Boy baby: "Shut up! You just rolled over on my pacifier."

•

What do you get from a midget cocksucker?
  A low blow.

•

A harelip enters a nut shop and spends about fifteen minutes perusing the display cases while the old Jewish proprietor watches silently. Finally the harelip asks, "Say, mister, these pistachios, how much are they?"

"Young man," answers the Jew, "pistachios are six dollars and thirty cents a pound."

"Six-thirty a pound!" exclaims the harelip. "That's way out of line. How much are your cashews?"

"Cashews, my friend, are four-eighty a pound."

"Holy smoke! I can't afford that. So tell me, how much are your cheapest peanuts?"

"All the way at the end we have peanuts in the shell for one-sixty a pound."

"Why, they're cheaper at the ball park!" cries the harelip. "You know something, mister," he adds, "I can't afford your prices, but it's nice that you haven't made fun of the way I talk."

"So why should I," responds the old Jew. "Everybody's got a little imperfection. Take me, I've been walking around with this schnozzola for the last sixty-eight years."

"Jesus Christ, is that your nose?" yells the harelip. "For a while there I thought it was your cock, your nuts are so high."

•

What's the height of cheapness?
  Taking an anorectic to dinner.

•

Why did the girl fall off the swing?
She didn't have any arms.

•

Why were the midget and the circus fat lady so deliriously happy when they got married?
She let him try out a new wrinkle every night.

•

The director of the local loony bin, Fred, and his assistant, Joe, decided to take ten of their best-behaved charges to a ball game. "Get up, nuts," said Fred when they arrived at the park, and they got up. "Off the bus, nuts," he said, and off they went, then, "Stand in line, nuts," and, once they had found their seats, "Sit down, nuts," and the nuts obeyed.

After a while Fred asked Joe to watch over the patients while he went to the men's room, figuring they were so well behaved that there wouldn't be any problem. But when he came back, there was a riot going on. "What the hell happened, Joe?" he asked.

"Well," said Joe, "one guy went by shouting, 'Hotdogs, hotdogs, hotdogs,' and another guy went by shouting, 'Popcorn, popcorn, popcorn,' and then another guy came by and yelled, 'Peanuts, peanuts, peanuts. . . .'"

•

What do you do when an epileptic has a seizure in your bathtub?
Start enjoying your new Jacuzzi.

•

What do you call a black male with no arms or legs, floating in the lake?
Buoy.

•

What do you call a girl who's just been run over by a truck?
  Patty.

•

How about a girl with one leg?
  Peg.

•

What do you call a girl with no arms and no legs in a cash register?
  Penny.

The same girl on a gambling table?
  Betsy.

The same girl on a music stand?
  Carol.

How about that girl working at a vineyard?
  Sherry.

•

And what do you call a girl that's taking downers?
  Barb.

•

A man with a bad stuttering problem had never married, but one day he met the woman of his dreams, a lovely young epileptic. After a whirlwind courtship, the two were married, and after the ceremony they headed for a honeymoon in the Poconos. Five minutes after they'd registered, the phone rang at the front desk.

"C-c-come q-q-quick and b-b-bring a r-r-rope," the man yelled into the manager's ear.

After a desperate search for a rope, the manager raced up the stairs. There on the bed, naked, was the wife in the midst of a seizure. The husband grabbed the rope from the manager, proceeded to tie her to the bed, and then climbed up on top of her.

"Okay," he shouted, "c-c-cut h-h-her l-l-loose!"

•

What has four wheels and flies?
   A dead cripple in a wheelchair.

•

Why didn't they let the midget in the nudist colony?
   He kept getting into everyone's hair.

•

How did the father call his deformed daughter to dinner?
   "Here, lip! Here, lip!"

•

Hold your arm straight out in front of you. Open your hand and turn it so the palm is perpendicular to the floor. Ask, "What am I?"

   Answer: a one-armed man describing the one that got away.

•

The anatomy lesson for the week was the way in which the body of a handicapped person compensates for its deficiencies. As an example, the professor showed a slide of a man with no legs whose arms and shoulders had consequently become hugely muscled. "Your assignment," he instructed a pretty medical student, "is to find someone who has compensated for a physical handicap and to report on it for the class."

After class the student went into the bar next door, and what should she catch sight of but a hunchback nursing a beer at the bar. Screwing up her courage, she went over and told him about her assignment. "If you don't mind my asking," she said sweetly, "is there some part of your anatomy which has compensated for your handicap?"

"As a matter of fact there is," said the hunchback. "Come up to my place and I'll show you." When they got upstairs, he dropped his pants and revealed the biggest cock she had ever seen. Kneeling down, she couldn't resist touching it, then caressing it, then rubbing it against her face.

"Jesus Christ, don't blow it!" screamed the hunchback, jumping back. "That's how I got the hump on my back."

•

Did you hear about the guy who lost the use of his whole left side?

He's all right now.

•

The foreman at the sawmill wasn't eager to hire the blind man because of the obvious risks involved, but the guy begged for a chance. "You'll see," he said. "Just put me downstream of the saw and I'll smell the type and length of the lumber and stack it accordingly."

So the foreman agreed to give it a shot. Positioning the blind man, he sent down a twelve-foot piece of pine. "Ah-hah," said the man, breathing deeply, "pine, twelve-foot," and stacked it in place. The foreman repeated the test with oak and redwood, fir and mahogany, and the guy didn't miss once. Then, getting a sly look on his face, the foreman sent for the office secretary, old Mabel, and told her to hike up her skirts and ride down the conveyor belt. Mabel rode through, faceup, right past the blind man. Sniffing furiously and looking very puzzled, he asked that the last piece of wood be sent through again. The foreman complied, but not before telling Mabel, skirts still up, to turn over.

After a few moments of reflection, the blind man turned to the foreman with a triumphant smile. "I've got it!" he proclaimed. "That's the shithouse door from a tuna boat!"

•

The bus driver was training a new kid to take over his route. At one stop a middle-aged woman was waiting, and when the driver waved to her, she waved back. She held up her index finger, at which the driver shook his head and held up his index and middle fingers. She pointed her thumb up, and the driver shook his head vigorously and pointed his thumb down. To the new kid's astonishment, the woman then started fondling her tits, to which the driver responded by scratching his balls. And the woman gave him the finger and walked off.

"What the hell was that all about?" asked the kid. "Was she crazy or something?"

"Nah," said the driver, "just deaf. See, she asked me if this was the number-one bus, and I told her it was the number two. She asked if we were going uptown, and I said no, downtown. Then she wanted to know if we were going to the Dairy Queen, and I said no, to the ball park. So she said, 'Fuck you, I'll walk.'"

CELEBRITIES

How does Linda Lovelace masturbate?
  (Clear your throat.)

●

What did Cleopatra say to Marc Antony?
  "Not tonight. I have my pyramid."

●

Did you hear that the girl who played Annie was on the set when Vic Morrow was hurt?
  She started singing, "Two Morrows, two Morrows. . . ."

●

Joe: "Did you hear about the dumb mosquito?"
  Sam: "No, I didn't."
  Joe: "He bit Dolly Parton on the arm."

●

What's cold and wants to hold your hand?
John Lennon.

•

Have you heard about Renée Richards' new book?
It's called *Tennis Without Balls*.

•

What's the difference between Karen Carpenter and Liberace?
One's a skeleton and one's in the closet.

•

Did you hear about the Olympic Committee's budget squeeze?
Instead of getting torchbearers, they're hiring Richard Pryor for a rerun.

•

Who makes the best Oriental vegetables?
Ray "Boom-boom" Mancini.

•

What happened to Buddy Holly's plane party?
It got crashed.

•

What's the difference between Adolf Hitler and a jockstrap?
One's a dictator and the other's a dicktoter.

•

Who makes Dolly Parton's bras?
Hefty—"tough enough to overstuff."

•

What was Barney Clark's last word?
  "Bleep!"

•

Did you hear about the new show starring Sylvester Stallone
and Dolly Parton?
  It's called "Rocky Mountains."

•

What's Prince?
  Living proof that Johnny Mathis screwed Michael Jackson.

•

What's brown and sits in the woods?
  Winnie's Pooh.

•

Did you hear that Indira Gandhi's assassination was really
an accident?
  The bodyguards were actually a couple of Poles trying to
blow a fly off her head.

•

How do you catch Dolly Parton in the jungle?
  Booby traps.

•

Which hand did Hitler use to wipe himself, his left or his
right?
  Neither—he used toilet paper. He wasn't *that* crazy.

•

What's Roman Polanski's favorite song?
"Thank Heaven for Little Girls."
And the runner-up?
"Baby Love."

.

How does Ozzie Osborne change a light bulb?
First he bites off the old one.

.

What do you get when you cross Boy George and Michael Jackson?
George Burns.

.

What's this: "Oooh, ooooh, yes, mmm, yes, mmmmm, mmm, pweeze, yes, yes, oooh, aaaaaaah. . . . Wuz I vewwy good?"
Elmer Fudd with a prostitute.

.

Have you read the new bestseller?
Thinner Thighs and Hips and Calves and Arms and Fingers and Toes and Back and Waist and Face in Thirty Days, by Karen Carpenter.

.

How does Jesse Jackson stand on abortion?
One foot on its stomach, one on its head.

.

What do you call a gay bathroom?
Elton John.

.

Why couldn't Joan of Arc go out with her French boyfriend?
　　She had a date with a Pole.

•

What's the difference between Willie Nelson and Dean Martin?
　　Willie Nelson is an older country-western singer, and Dean Martin is a singer older than most Western countries.

•

Why did Bobby Sands' wife divorce him?
　　He wouldn't eat her.

•

What's brown and hides in the attic?
　　Diarrhea of Anne Frank.

•

What was Humpty Dumpty's last thought?
　　"Oh, my God, I'm not wearing clean underwear!"

•

What did the doctor tell Rock Hudson when he contracted AIDS?
　　"Don't worry, you'll be back on your knees in no time."

•

Hear about the new movie starring Sylvester Stallone and Rock Hudson?
　　It's called "Rambutt."

•

Who was the unluckiest person in the world?
  The last person to get a piece of the Rock.

•

Did you hear that Rock Hudson got food poisoning?
  He ate a bad wienie.

•

What's white and has a black asshole?
  The A-Team.

•

What does PLO stand for?
  Push Leon Overboard.

•

And how do you know the Israelis didn't do it?
  They would have sold the wheelchair.

•

Did you hear about the Klinghoffer cocktail?
  Two shots and a splash.

•

Do you know why Hitler committed suicide?
  He got the gas bill.

•

Who did Ronald Reagan send to Rock Hudson's funeral?
  His aides.

•

What do Reagan and a typewriter have in common?
  Semicolons.

•

Why couldn't Rock Hudson get auto insurance?
  He'd been rear-ended too often.

•

Did you hear about Evil Knievel's latest stunt?
  He's going to run across Ethiopia with a sandwich tied to his back.

•

Why did they put Rock Hudson in his casket facedown?
  So all his friends could recognize him.

•

Why doesn't Rock Hudson know who gave him AIDS?
  He doesn't have eyes in the back of his head.

•

What do you get when you cross a cat with Mick Jagger?
  A pussy with big lips.

•

What kind of car does Renée Richards drive?
  A convertible.

•

Did you hear about the Richard Simmons doll?
  Wind it up and it ignores Barbie and asks Ken out for a drink.

•

Whose autograph is this?*

*See page 110 for answer.

STILL EVEN MORE JOKES FOR THE BLIND
(back by popular demand)

MALE ANATOMY

One day a young woman was walking home when a man grabbed her, dragged her into a back alley, and started molesting her. "Help! Help me, someone," she cried. "I'm being robbed!"

"You ain't being robbed, lady," interrupted the man, "you're being screwed."

"Well, if this is being screwed," she said, "I'm being robbed."

•

What's a baby before it's born?
  Daddy's little squirt.

•

How do you quit masturbation?
  Cold jerky.

•

Girl in Music Store: "Have you got Hot Lips on a ten-inch Decca?"

Clerk: "No, but I've got hot nuts on a nine-inch pecker."

Girl: "Is that a record?"

Clerk: "No, but it's better than average."

•

Did you hear about the new male hygiene deodorant called Umpire?

It gets rid of foul balls.

•

Why is a bachelor skinny and a married man fat?

The bachelor comes home, sees what's in the refrigerator, and goes to bed. The married man comes home, sees what's in the bed, and goes to the refrigerator.

•

"In return for releasing me from my imprisonment in that cursed bottle," said grateful Gina the genie to Paul the pauper, "I hereby grant you three wishes—however, your worst enemy will get twice what you do."

"Fine with me," agreed Paul. "For my first wish, I'd like to be rich beyond my wildest dreams." Immediately, he was surrounded by caskets of precious stones, gold bullion, and negotiable securities.

"There you go," said Gina. "But your worst enemy now has a hoard that would put J. Paul Getty and all the Rocke- fellers to shame."

"That's okay. For my second wish, I'd like a harem of the world's most beautiful and alluring women ready to fulfill my every desire." And—poof!—a bevy of beauties sur- rounded him, giggling and fluttering their eyelashes.

"But your worst enemy now has a harem that would put Sheik Yamani to shame," pointed out the genie.

"That's okay," said Paul, grinning. "For my third wish, I'd like *one* of my testicles to disappear."

•

What's the definition of a skyjacking?
   A hand job at thirty-three thousand feet.

•

Why do men shake their cocks after they piss?
   Because they can't train them to go *sniff*.

•

Three guys were walking down the street when they were
suddenly stopped by a crazed addict who jumped out in
front of them. "You better have ten inches of dick between
the three of you, or I might have to have some fun with my
knife," he said, pulling out a switchblade.
   The first guy coolly whipped out his five-incher. The second guy wasn't far behind with his four-incher, and the third
produced his one-incher. Satisfied, the junkie let them go.
   The three headed off around the corner, where the first
guy gasped, "Good thing I had my five-incher."
   The second guy said, "Yeah, and we're lucky I had my
four inches."
   "No kidding," said the third guy. "Thank God I had a
hard-on!"

•

Why do guys sleep better on their sides?
   They have a kickstand.

•

Two very nervous young men got to talking in the doctor's
waiting room and discovered they had similar symptoms.
One had a red ring around the base of his penis and the
other one a green ring. The fellow with the red ring was
examined first. In a few minutes he came out, all smiles, and
said, "Don't worry, man, it's nothing!"
   Vastly relieved, the second patient went into the examining room, only to be told a few minutes later by the doctor,

"I'm very sorry, but you have an advanced case of VD and your penis will have to be amputated."

Turning white as a sheet, the young man gasped, "But the first guy . . . he said it was no big deal!"

"Well, you know," said the doctor, "there's a big difference between gangrene and lipstick."

•

What do you do with 365 used rubbers?

Make them into a tire and call it a Goodyear.

•

A woman went into the neighborhood grocery store and asked the grocer for a can of cat food. Knowing that she didn't have a cat, the grocer asked why she was buying the stuff. "It's for my husband's lunch," was the answer.

Shocked, the grocer said, "You can't feed cat food to your husband. It'll kill him!"

"I've been giving it to him for a week now and he likes it fine," was her answer, and each day the woman continued to come in and purchase a can of cat food for her husband's lunch.

It wasn't too much later that the grocer happened to be scanning the obituary column in the local paper and noticed that the woman's husband had passed away. When the woman came into the store, he couldn't resist saying, "I'm sorry to hear about your husband, but I warned you that he'd die if you kept feeding him cat food."

"It wasn't the food that killed him," she retorted. "He broke his neck trying to lick his ass!"

•

What begins with F, ends in K, and can easily be replaced if it doesn't work?

A fork.

•

A man who had problems with premature ejaculation went to a sex shop for a remedy. The clerk handed him a little yellow can and said, "This is Stay-Hard Spray; put on a little and you can go all night!"

Delighted, the guy took it home, stowed it on the cellar shelf, and waited eagerly for bedtime, when he sprayed some on his dick and went upstairs to his wife. But it seemed to make him come quicker than ever. The next day he returned to the sex shop, slammed the can down on the counter, and snapped, "This stuff makes me worse than before!"

Reading the label, the clerk asked, "Did you hide this stuff on the cellar shelf?"

"Yeah, so?" said the disgruntled customer.

"You must have grabbed the wrong can. This is Easy-Off."

•

What do pitchers and gigolos have in common?
    Fast balls.

•

Harry stopped by the funeral parlor to see his friend Joe, who was an embalmer, and found him at work on a corpse with a gigantic penis. The man's apparatus was so spectacular that Harry blurted out, "Wouldn't I love to have that cock!"

"You might as well—this guy doesn't need it anymore," said Joe, and he proceeded to cut off the organ and hand it to Harry. Harry wrapped it up carefully and took it home, where he found his wife in the kitchen making dinner. Deciding to have a little fun, Harry unwrapped the package, stuck it between his legs, and rushed into the kitchen, shouting, "Look, honey, look!"

His wife took one look and asked, "What happened to Sidney?"

•

What goes, "Ha! Ha! Thump! Thump!"?
A man laughing his balls off.

•

"Why do you iron your bra when you have nothing to put into it?" asked the husband snidely.
"I iron your shorts, don't I?" retorted the wife.

•

What does the perfect male look like?
Long, dark, and handsome.

•

New male horror movie: "Chain Saw Vasectomy."

•

Why did the girl blow her lover after sex?
She wanted to have her cock and eat it too.

•

The patient cleared his throat a little embarrassedly before explaining his rather unusual problem. "YOU SEE, DOC," he boomed in a voice so deep and raspy it was almost impossible to understand, "I CAN'T GO ON WITH THIS VOICE ANYMORE—IT'S DRIVING ME CRAZY. CAN YOU FIX IT SO I SOUND LIKE A NORMAL PERSON?"

"I'll certainly try," said the doctor. After examining the patient, he reported that some sort of weight was pulling on the vocal cords and distorting the voice. "Any idea what it could be?" he queried.

The patient cleared his throat again. "ACTUALLY, DOC, I HAPPEN TO BE . . . UH . . . ESPECIALLY WELL ENDOWED, AND MAYBE THAT'S WHAT'S DOING IT. LISTEN, IF YOU HAVE TO REMOVE

SOME OF IT, THAT'S FINE BY ME. I'LL DO *ANYTHING* TO GET A VOICE LIKE A REGULAR GUY." So the doctor went ahead and performed the operation.

Two weeks later the patient telephoned the doctor's office. "Hey, Doc," he babbled happily, "I can't thank you enough. Finally I sound like everyone else—it's just great!" After a pause, he asked, "Say, by the way, what'd you do with the piece of my penis you removed?"

"I THREW IT AWAY," said the doctor.

•

What's the definition of "dumb"?

A guy who rolls up his sleeve when a girl says she wants to feel his muscle.

•

Explaining to his doctor that his sex life wasn't all it could be, Milt asked for a pill that would enable him to get it up for his wife. It so happened that the doctor had just the right medication, so Milt took a pill and drove home. But when he got to the apartment his wife wasn't at home, and after waiting for an hour or so in growing discomfort, Milt finally had to jerk off.

When the doctor called to check the next day, Milt explained what had happened. "Well, gee, Milt, you didn't have to do for yourself," pointed out the doctor. "There are other women in the building."

"Doctor," said Milt, "for other women I don't need a pill."

•

Did you hear about the butcher who got behind in his work?

He backed into the meat grinder.

•

What's a midget's circumcision?
A Tiny Trim.

•

The chief bosun's mate took advantage of any opportunity to bully the crew. When they returned to port, it was time to paint the boat, and the mate had a fine time shouting down at the hapless sailors suspended over the side.

"Milligan," he bawled at one unfortunate, "you paint like I fuck!"

"I see, sir," said Milligan, looking up. "Did I get it on my face?"

•

After the wedding, young Ramona was taken upstairs by her groom, but after less than a minute she came running downstairs to the kitchen where her mother was making lasagna. "Mama, Mama," the young virgin wailed, "he's got hair all over his chest!"

"He's-a supposed to have hair on his chest," her mother replied calmly. "Now go back upstairs."

A few minutes later Ramona ran into the kitchen again. "Mama, he's got hair all over his legs!"

"He's-a supposed to, Ramona. Now go back upstairs like a good girl."

But when her groom took off his shoes and socks, Ramona saw that while one foot was normal, the other was a clubfoot. Faster than ever she raced down the stairs and yelled, "Mama, Mama, he's got half a foot."

"You stay here and cook-a the lasagna," said Mama, drying off her hands. "I'm-a going upstairs."

FEMALE ANATOMY

Mrs. Jones was quite startled when her six-year-old son barged into the bathroom just as she was stepping out of the shower. She hastily covered up, but not before the little boy pointed right at her crotch and asked, "What's that?"

"Oh," she said, thinking fast, "that's where I got hit with an ax."

"Got you right in the cunt, didn't it?"

•

Why is virginity like a balloon?
  One prick and they're both gone.

•

Why did the woman put a candle in her navel?
  Her lover liked to eat by candlelight.

•

One summer evening in New York a pretty girl was walking across Broadway and was hit by a truck. The impact was so strong that she flew up into the air, and by the time she hit the ground all her clothes had been stripped away.

As a crowd started to gather, a passing priest who had witnessed the accident rushed over and placed his hat over the victim's crotch so as to preserve a little decency.

Soon a drunkard, wondering what was going on, staggered through the crowd and caught sight of the naked girl lying in the street, covered only by the priest's hat. "Oh, Christ," he mumbled, "first thing we have to do is get that man out of there."

•

Why are pregnant women like defective typewriters?
   They skip their periods.

•

What's the definition of feminine deodorant spray?
   Around-the-cock protection.

•

What's an 11?
   A 10 that swallows.

•

A woman went to apply for a job as a truck driver. Not too keen on the idea, the personnel manager for the trucking company said, "You have to be pretty tough to cut it as a truck driver, you know."

"I'm tough, I really am," said the eager applicant.

"Well, do you drink and smoke?"

"Yes, of course."

"Do you cuss a lot?" asked the interviewer.

"You bet," said the woman. "I cuss like a lumberjack."

"So have you ever been picked up by the fuzz?"

"Well, no," she admitted, "but I've been swung around by the tits a couple of times."

•

What's better than a cold Budweiser?
A warm Busch.

•

What's the German word for "virgin"?
Goesintight.

•

And the German word for "Vaseline"?
Derwienerslider.

•

How about the Russian word for "VD"?
Rotchercockoff.

•

This guy screwed a hooker and spent his last dime on her. Only at the end did he realize he was penniless, so he asked if he could borrow the dime so he could get home on the bus. "Sure," she said, "if you eat it out of my twat."

So the man got down on his hands and knees and went to work, and after a few minutes he said, "I got it. See ya." A little while later his bus pulled up, and he dropped his fare in the token box and sat down.

The bus driver turned around and hollered, "Hey, buddy, how far do you think you're going to get on that scab?"

•

Did you hear the new slogan for Clairol hair color?
"Buy a double batch and get a snatch to match!"

•

Did you hear about the prostitute with a degree in psychology?

She'll blow your mind.

•

The gynecologist stuck up his head after completing his examination. "I'm sorry, miss," he said, "but removing that vibrator is going to involve a very lengthy and delicate operation."

"I'm not sure I can afford it," sighed the young woman on the examining table. "Why don't you just replace the batteries?"

•

Why is the new contraceptive sponge such a great idea?

Because after sex your wife can get up and wash the dishes.

•

Did you hear about the woman who shaved her legs and rectum?

•

It seems there was this woman who hated wearing underwear. One day she decided to go shopping for a new pair of shoes, and since she was wearing a skirt the salesman was enjoying an excellent view. After the third or fourth pair of shoes, the guy couldn't stand it anymore. "Lady," he said, "that's some beautiful sight. I could eat that pussy full of ice cream."

Disgusted, the woman ran out of the store and went home. When her husband got home from work, she told him about the incident and asked him to go beat the shit out of the salesman. And when he flatly refused, she wanted to know why.

"Three reasons," said her husband. "Number one, you

shouldn't have been out in a skirt with no underpants. Number two, you have enough shoes to last you ten more years. And number three, any motherfucker who can eat that much ice cream I don't want to mess with in the first place."

•

What are the three best things about being a woman?
   You can bleed without cutting yourself.
   You can bury a bone without digging a hole.
   And you can make a man come without calling him.

•

What's a female Taurus?
   A Clitaurus, of course.

•

Did you hear about the woman who injected herself with a mixture of chicken and rabbit hormones?
   Now she can cluck like a bunny.

•

If God made the top half of a woman, who made the bottom?
   A black. Who else would give it big lips, kinky hair, and a smell like a catfish?

•

Three black women decided to share an apartment, and by coincidence they all had boyfriends named Leroy. After a week, things got so confusing that they decided to give each man a nickname from a brand of soda. The first woman said, "I'll name mine Mountain Dew, because he lives on a mountain and he loves to do, do, do!"
   "I'll name mine Seven-Up," spoke up the second, "be-

cause he's seven inches long and he's always up."

The third woman thought for a while, then said, "I'll name mine Jack Daniel's."

"That's not a soda," pointed out her roommates, "that's a liquor."

She smiled. "That's my Leroy."

•

What's a corporate virgin?

Someone who's new to the firm.

•

There was a young girl who was eating a chocolate-chip cookie during her haircut. "You're getting hair on your cookie," pointed out the hairdresser.

"I know," she said, "and my titties are getting big too."

•

Mabel had tried every diet plan in the world to no avail and finally had to agree that some sort of daily exercise was required if she was going to lose weight. Her doctor suggested a program of calisthenics, and Mabel dutifully started in "bicycling" with her feet in the air, only to find that her pants were so tight that she couldn't complete the exercise. So Mabel decided to try it in the nude, but, oh, those rug burns. Finally she tried doing the exercise on her bed, and it worked fine.

Unfortunately, a few days into the program Mabel threw her legs over her head so energetically that they got caught in her wrought-iron headboard. Mabel was well and truly stuck and could do nothing but moan for help until her husband got home from work. Hearing her feeble groans, he sauntered into the bedroom, only to exclaim, "Why, Mabel, if you'd put your teeth in and comb your hair, you'd look just like your mother!"

•

A hooker went into the bank to put away some newly acquired earrings. "I happen to know something about jewelry, madam," confided the teller, "and I hope you know that these are not genuine diamonds."

"Oh, my God!" screamed the hooker. "I've been raped."

•

One night Jerry brought home a dozen roses to his wife. "How lovely, dear," she said. "What's the occasion?"

"I want to make love to you," he said simply.

"Not tonight, dear. I have a headache."

The next night Jerry came home with a big box of chocolates and explained that he wanted to make love with her.

"I'm awfully tired, honey," said his wife. "Not tonight."

Every night for a week Jerry brought home something, but each time his wife's answer was no. Finally he came home with six black kittens with little red bows around their necks and handed them to his wife. "How adorable, Jerry," she exclaimed. "But what are they for?"

"These are six little pallbearers for your dead pussy."

•

What's the difference between a sewing machine and a lady jogger?

A sewing machine has only one bobbin.

•

One night little Johnny walked in on his parents while they were screwing. "Daddy," he cried, "what are you and Mommy doing?"

"Uh . . . we're making a little sister for you to play with," stammered his father.

"Oh, neat," said Johnny, and went back to bed.

The next day his dad came home to find the little boy sobbing his eyes out on the front porch. "What's wrong, Johnny?" he asked, picking him up.

"You know the little sister you and Mommy made me?"

"Yes," said his father, blushing.

The little boy wailed, "Today the milkman ate it."

•

What giggles and smokes like a chimney?

A white woman in heat.

•

Rick was trying real hard to get the best-looking cheerleader in school to go out on a date with him. She finally agreed, but only on condition that he arrange a date for her best friend too. That was fine with Rick, but when Friday night came around, he hadn't been able to line anyone up so he asked his retarded brother, Bill, if he would help him out.

"Why, sure," said Bill, "but you know, I've never been out with a girl before."

"No problem," said Rick. "Just do everything I do."

Off the four of them went to the drive-in, and when Rick started kissing his date, Bill followed suit. Soon Rick had the cheerleader's bra undone, so Rick undid his date's. Next, Rick was feeling inside her panties, but when Bill tried to follow suit, his date told him to quit.

"Why?" asked Bill, anxiously noting that his brother was getting quite a head start in the back seat.

"I have my period," she said.

"Your what?"

"I'm bleeding down there," she explained, blushing.

"This I gotta see," said Bill. He turned on the headlights, dragged his date out in front of the car, pulled down her pants, and said, "Hell, I'd be bleeding too if my dick was chopped off!"

•

Who are the six most important men in a woman's life?

The doctor: He says, "Take your clothes off."

The dentist: He says, "Open wide."

The hairdresser: He says, "Do you want it teased or blown?"

The interior decorator: He says, "You'll like it once it's in."

The milkman: He says, "Do you want it in front or in back?"

The banker: He says, "If you take it out, you'll lose interest."

•

Toast at a bachelor party:

> Here's to the hole
>   that never heals.
> The more you rub it
>   the better it feels.
> Not all the soap
>   and water in hell
> Can wash away
>   that fishy smell.

•

This guy is out on a date with a girl, and they end up back at his apartment on the couch with the lights off. Suddenly, to his horror his hairpiece falls off and he begins to grope around in the dark for it.

Not realizing what's happened, his date begins cooing passionately. "That's it, honey," she whispers, "right there. You've got it . . . you've got it now. . . ."

"No, I don't," he says, sitting up and looking at her. "My rug isn't parted in the middle."

•

Did you hear about the woman who was so ugly that when she was born, the doctor slapped her mother?

•

There's this whore who got all gussied up every Saturday night to make the rounds of the bars. She said she would give any man five hundred dollars if he could make a rhyme to rhyme with hers:

> Three plus three is six,
> Six plus three is nine,
> I can guess the length of yours
> But you can't guess the depth of mine.

She did this for about a month and nobody could match her rhyme. So late one Saturday night she was walking home alone when she came across a drunk. She made him the same offer, and after scratching his head and thinking for a minute, the guy said, "I got it:

> Three plus three may be six
> And six plus three may be nine,
> I bet you I can piss in yours
> But you can't piss in mine!"

•

A well-built guy and his gorgeous date came out of the movie theater and strolled down to the neighborhood coffeehouse. As they stepped inside, the regulars swiveled around on their seats to check out the newcomers and then turned back to their conversations—with one notable exception. This one fellow was ogling the woman with bulging eyes and tongue hanging out, practically drooling on his shirtfront.

Enraged by his crude behavior, the woman's date walked over, grabbed the ogler by his shirt collar, and shook him like a dishrag. "I'll teach you to stare at my woman with those filthy thoughts written all over your ugly face," he bellowed. "Any more ideas like that come into your mind and I'll slice you up like salami."

"Please, sir," pleaded the terrified ogler, "I truly meant no offense. I assure you I wasn't entertaining any sort of impure thoughts, just admiring your taste in female companionship." Somewhat mollified, the man slowly released his grip on the shirt collar.

Straightening his shirt, the voyeur went on in a more confident tone of voice, "In fact, if you'd care to have a seat, I'd be delighted to buy you both a cup of pussy."

HOMOSEXUALS

Two gays were walking down the street in San Francisco when a man walked past them. "See that guy?" said one fag to the other. "He's a great fuck!"

"No shit!" exclaimed his friend.

"Well, hardly any."

•

What do you get when you cross a gay guy and a dick?

Sticky fingers.

•

A flaming fag sashays into the roughest truckstop on the highway, a parakeet on his shoulder. He looks around the restaurant at all the burly truckers and announces loudly, "Whichever one of you big bruisers can guess the weight of this darling parakeet gets to go home with me."

Silence falls over the truckstop. Then one of the toughest-looking guys speaks up. "That's an easy one—five hundred pounds."

The fag shrieks delightedly, "We have a winner! We have a winner!"

•

Did you hear about Ben Hur's sex-change operation? Now he's called Ben Gay.

•

What do you call a gay person from the Deep South? A homosex-you-all.

•

Why do fags become paleontologists? To find a *Homo erectus*.

•

A gay goes to the proctologist for a routine examination. When the doctor gets him into position, he's quite surprised to find a piece of string dangling from the man's ass. He pulls gently on the string and out pops a lovely bouquet of flowers.

"Do you know I just pulled a dozen roses out of your rectum?" asks the astonished doctor.

"Is that so?" said the patient. "Who're they from?"

•

What was the gay rapist charged with? Homo-cide.

•

How many gay people does it take to change a light bulb? Two. One to screw the bulb and the other to grease the socket.

•

Two fags were walking down the street and the first one said, "Hold it a sec—I smell fresh cock."

"No, you don't," said his companion. "I just burped."

•

Why do gays make lousy Santas?
Instead of filling your stockings, they try them on.

•

Why don't fags lean on baseball bats?
They're afraid it might get too serious.

•

Two gays were having a drink at the bar when an attractive woman walked by. "Mmmmmm. . . ." said one appreciatively, eyeing her up and down.

"Oh, Tom!" shrieked his horrified friend. "Don't tell me you're going straight!"

"Nothing like that," said Tom musingly. "It's just that sometimes I can't help wishing I'd been born a lesbian. . . ."

•

Did you hear that the fag canceled his ocean cruise?
He heard that Moby Dick was a whale.

•

What do you get when you cross Father Damien with Fire Island?
An AIDS colony.

•

A fag was brushing his teeth when his gums started bleeding. "Thank God," he mumbled, "safe for another month."

•

Two young gay lovers were fighting:
  "Drop dead!"
  "Go to hell!"
  "Kiss my ass!"
  "Oh, so you wanna make up!"

•

What's a gay mafioso?
  A fairy godfather.

•

What charges can you bring against a transvestite?
  Male fraud.

•

One fine day a cowboy walked into a bar and said to the
bartender, "I'll bet you a tall, cold beer that my pet alligator
here can suck my cock."

  "Okay, wiseguy, you got a deal," said the bartender.

  The cowboy pulled out a long switch and slapped the alligator across its snout and opened his fly. Sure enough the
alligator proceeded to slowly open his mouth and suck the
cowboy's cock, slow and easy.

  "Okay, you win the bet," said the bartender, "but I want
to see it one more time."

  One tap of the switch and the alligator went through his
paces again. After three more performances, the cowboy
turned to the amazed spectators and asked if there was anyone else who'd like to try it for themselves.

  "I'll give it a shot," said a fag in the corner, "but only if
you promise not to slap me with the switch."

•

What's "tender love"?
  A pair of homosexuals with hemorrhoids.

•

Did you hear about the gay law firm?
    They get into each other's briefs and play with their sub-
poenas.

•

Graffiti:
    "My mother made me a homosexual."
    "If I give her the yarn, will she make me one too?"

•

How come gays are good basketball players?
    They can make a good swish.

•

Did you hear about the gay Bible?
    The first couple was Adam and Steve.

•

What happened when the two gay sergeants met?
    They talked about their privates.

•

Gay man to whore: "Prostitute!"
    Whore to gay man: "Substitute!"

•

Why do transvestites like Christmas?
    That's when they don their gay apparel.

•

How can you tell a macho fag at the beach?
    By the shaving scars on his legs.

•

What do gay South Africans get?
  Apart-AIDS.

•

Two fags were arguing:
  "Butter!"
  "Margarine!"
  "Butter!"
  "Margarine!"
  The first fag sighed. "Okay, darling, we'll compromise—
let's use Vaseline."

•

What's another name for AIDS?
  Toxic cock syndrome.

•

This is a fairy tale:
  Once upon a time there was a rich and handsome king.
He sent fliers throughout his kingdom promising that who-
ever brought him the head of the fearsome dragon that was
terrorizing the countryside could have all of his wealth or
the hand of his lovely daughter in marriage. Of course, all
the able-bodied men in the kingdom went off in pursuit.
Three days later a fellow arrived at the palace door bearing
the bloody head of the dragon. "Well done," exclaimed the
king. "You may have my beautiful daughter's hand."
  "Thanks, but I don't want your daughter," said the man.
  "I see. Come with me to empty out the treasury," offered
the king.
  "Thanks, but I don't want your money either. I want
YOU, sweetie!" So they lived happily ever after.
  See, I *told* you it was a fairy tale.

•

How do you get rid of crabs?
  Find a cocksucker who likes seafood.

•

What do you call a homosexual's athletic supporter?
  A fruit cup.

•

Know how you get hearing AIDS?
  From listening to assholes.

RELIGIOUS

Begin invited the Pope to play golf. Since the Pope had no idea how to play, he convened the College of Cardinals to ask their advice. "Call Jack Nicklaus," they suggested, "and let him play in your place. Tell Begin you're sick or something."

Honored by His Holiness's request, Nicklaus agreed to represent him on the links. John Paul, again with advice from his staff, made him a cardinal just in case Begin was to get suspicious.

When Nicklaus returned from the match, the Pope asked him how he had done. "I came in second," was the reply.

"You mean to tell me Begin beat you?" John Paul yelled.

"No, Your Holiness," said Jack. "Rabbi Palmer did."

•

How do the Catholics make money during the hot summer months?

They freeze the holy water and sell it as Popesicles.

•

What do you do with a worn-out bra?

Use it as a skullcap for Siamese-twin rabbis.

•

The Pope sent an urgent telegram to all his cardinals, saying: "Drop everything and get to Rome on the double!"

When they arrived, he called them together and said, "I've some good news and some bad news. First the good news—God called me on the phone to tell me the world was going to end next month and we'd better get ready."

A nervous hush came over the audience. In the back of the hall, a cardinal meekly asked, "But, Your Holiness, if that is the good news, what could the bad news possibly be?"

"He was calling from Salt Lake City."

•

What do you get when you cross a Mormon and an Indian?

A basement full of stolen groceries.

•

"Someone stole my bike," complained a priest to his minister friend.

"Bring up the Ten Commandments in your sermon tomorrow, and as soon as you mention 'Thou shalt not steal' the guilty party will come forward," the minister said confidently.

The next day the priest visited the minister and happily reported he'd found his bike. "Yes," he went on, "when I came to 'Thou shalt not commit adultery,' I remembered where I'd left it."

•

A young Irishman had recently been ordained as a priest and was traveling to his new parish in the Irish countryside. As he drove down the lane, he saw a man in the ditch at the side of the road, fucking a sheep. The young priest shuddered, uttered a prayer, and crossed himself.

A few miles down the road he saw another man out in the fields frenziedly screwing a sheep. Appalled at having witnessed a second case of bestiality in less than an hour, he whispered several prayers, crossed himself fervently, and drove on.

Finally, on the outskirts of town, he caught sight of a man leaning against a tree and masturbating enthusiastically. The young priest, then and there, decided grimly on the topic of his first sermon.

"As I approached this fair town," he began that Sunday, "I witnessed three abominations. First, on the roadside a man committing an unnatural act with a sheep! Shortly thereafter was another man in a field committing the same unnatural act with another sheep! And third, at the very outskirts of this town, a man was committing an unnatural act with himself!"

A voice spoke up from somewhere in the congregation, "Aye, that'll be old Paddy Fitzpatrick. He never could catch a sheep."

•

Why is there a corner tap by the basilica?
So the Pope can cash his check too.

•

What's black and white and black and white and black and white?
A priest and nun screwing.

•

(Stand with feet together, arms outstretched as if being crucified, and look downward.)
"Scat! Shoo! Get the hell out of here! Go on! Beat it!"
(Slowly fall sideways.)
"Damn those beavers!"

•

What do you call a nun in a blender?
  Twisted Sister.

•

What's white, spotted, and gooey and rains down from the sky?
  The Coming of the Lord.

•

Little Johnny was going down the sidewalk when his wagon got caught in the mud. He was cussing up a storm when the neighborhood policeman came by and told him he'd better cut it out. When Johnny wanted to know why, the cop explained that God was everywhere.

  "Even in the back of my wagon?" asked the little boy.

  "Even in the back of your wagon, son," the cop assured him.

  "Well, then," said Johnny, "tell him to get off his ass and help push!"

•

Three men die on the same day and go to heaven. One by one they are interviewed by Saint Peter, who asks the first man how many times he's had sex. "Never. I'm a virgin," is the first guy's answer. Saint Peter gives him a Mercedes-Benz to get around in, and poses the same question to the second man. "Only once," he says, "on my wedding night." Giving him the keys to a Toyota, Saint Peter turns and asks the third man how often he's had sex in his life. "I've gotten laid so many times I've lost count," the fellow confesses. And Saint Peter gives him a bicycle.

  Not too much later the first man is tooling around in his Mercedes-Benz when he sees something so extraordinary that he turns his head to look, something so shocking that he is unable to avert his gaze. He crashes headlong into a tree, and when he comes to in Heaven Hospital, the angel doctors and police are standing by his bedside, waiting to find out what caused the accident. "It was shocking . . . simply shocking," whispers the poor man. "I . . . I . . . I saw Pope John Paul on roller skates!"

•

"Sister Bernadette, aren't you putting on a little weight?" inquired Father Flanagan during his visit to the convent, suspiciously eyeing her bulging stomach.

"Why, no, Father," answered the nun demurely, "it's just a little gas."

A few months later Father Flanagan put the same question to the nun, noticing that her habit barely fit across her belly.

"Oh, just a bit of gas," said Sister Bernadette, blushing a bit.

On his next visit Father Flanagan was walking down the corridor when he passed Sister Bernadette wheeling a baby carriage. Looking in, the priest observed, "Cute little fart."

•

When the Eisenbergs moved to Rome, little Hymie came home from school in tears. He explained to his mother that the nuns were always asking these Catholic questions and how was he, a nice Jewish boy, supposed to know the answers?

Mrs. Eisenberg's heart swelled with maternal sympathy, and she determined to help her son out. "Hymie," she said, "I'm going to embroider the answers on the inside of your shirt, and you just look down and read them the next time those nuns pick on you."

"Thanks, Mom," said Hymie, and he didn't bat an eye when Sister Michael asked him who the world's most famous virgin was. "Mary," he answered.

"Very good," said the nun. "And who was her husband?"

"Joseph," answered the boy.

"I see you've been studying. Now can you tell me the name of their son?"

"Sure," said Hymie. "Calvin Klein."

•

After many unbroken years of service to the priest of the parish, an old nun decided to take a vacation at the seaside. Wanting to make sure the priest was looked after as well as possible, she gave a young sister detailed instructions on every aspect of his care.

When the young nun came in on the first morning with the priest's breakfast, he told her he had a key between his legs and she had a lock between hers. "If I put my key in your lock," he explained to the girl, "it will open the gates to heaven." She thought that sounded like a fine idea, and they did it many times before the old nun came back to resume her duties.

On her return she asked how things had worked out, and the young sister eagerly explained about the gates of heaven. "Why, that lying old bastard!" shrieked the nun. "Thirty years ago he told me that was Gabriel's horn, and I've been blowing it ever since!"

CRUELTY TO ANIMALS

Two guys were walking down the street when they came across a dog sitting on the sidewalk, studiously licking its balls.

"Would I ever like to do that," sighed one man enviously.

"Go right ahead," encouraged his friend. "But if I were you, I'd pat him first."

•

Why does an elephant have four feet?
Because six inches isn't enough.

•

Since little Mortie had grown up on a farm, he was accustomed to screwing the cows, and it didn't bother his father until the lad turned fifteen and still didn't seem to be displaying any interest in girls. So Pa went into town and hired a beautiful prostitute for the evening. Following his directions, she went into the barn, took off all her clothes, and

82

went over to where the farm boy was standing on a wheel-barrow screwing a big Holstein.

"Say there, Mortie," said the woman seductively, "any-thing I can do for you?"

Mortie looked over at her and answered, "Sure—you can wheel me over to the next cow."

•

You already know how to make a dog sound like a cat and a cat sound like a dog (see TRULY TASTELESS JOKES IV), so how do you make a sheep sound like a cheerleader?

Put a bomb under her and light the fuse—she'll go "Ssssss, BOOM, baaaaaaa!"

•

If an elephant's front legs were going sixty miles per hour, what would its back legs be doing?

Hauling ass.

•

What does Miss Piggy use for a douche?

Hog wash.

•

Two ants met in this woman's belly button and decided to explore the rest of her body. Agreeing to meet again in a week, one ant headed north while the other went south.

Seven days later, they returned to the belly button. "I had a great time," reported the ant who had ventured north. "There were these two big hills, and every day I went skiing, and at night I slept in this nice warm valley."

"I had a hell of a time," sighed the other ant. "First I had to walk through this thick jungle, then I fell down this huge hole, and by the time I climbed out, I was so tired that I fell asleep in this smelly cave. But that wasn't the worst of it:

every night this giant worm came in and threw up in my face."

•

What did the elephant say to the naked man?
  "Cute! But can you eat peanuts with it?"

•

How do you find a rathole?
  Lift its tail.

•

In the middle of preparing dinner, a housewife discovered her blender wasn't working, so she asked her husband if he could fix it. After opening the back of the machine, he shook a large, very dead cockroach out onto the counter.
  "There's your problem," he announced. "The engineer died."

•

What do you get when you pour boiling hot water down a rabbit hole?
  Hot, cross bunnies.

•

A farmer was extolling the virtues of pig fucking to his neighbor and urging him to give it a try. Finally, after hours of convincing, the neighbor agreed to mount one of his sows.
  "I don't know, Clem," the neighbor reported, "I didn't enjoy that too much."
  "No wonder, Clyde," the farmer laughed, "you picked the ugliest one!"

•

What do you get when you cross a rat with an elephant?
   A dead rat with an eighteen-inch asshole.

•

How do you have fun with a dead hamster?
   Tie its tail to the exercise wheel and give it a spin.

•

This guy went to the zoo one day. While he was standing in front of the gorilla's enclosure, the wind gusted and he got some grit in his eye. As he pulled his eyelid down to dislodge the particle, the gorilla went crazy, bent open the bars, and beat the hapless fellow senseless. When the guy came to, the zookeeper was anxiously bending over him, and as soon as he was able to talk, he explained what had happened. The zookeeper nodded sagely and explained that in gorilla language, pulling down your eyelid meant "fuck you."

   The explanation didn't make the gorilla's victim feel any better, and he vowed revenge. The next day he purchased two large knives, two party hats, two party horns, and a large sausage. Putting the sausage in his pants, he hurried to the zoo and over to the gorilla's cage, into which he tossed a hat, a knife, and a party horn. Knowing that the big apes were natural mimics, he put on a party hat. The gorilla looked at him, looked at the hat, and put it on. Next he picked up his horn and blew on it. The gorilla picked up his horn and did the same. Then the man picked up his knife, whipped the sausage out of his pants, and sliced it neatly in two.

   The gorilla looked at the knife in his cage, looked at his own crotch, and solemnly pulled down his eyelid.

•

The first-grade class gathered around the teacher for a game of "Guess the Animal." The first picture the teacher held up was of a cat. "Okay, boys and girls," she said brightly, "can anyone tell me what this is?"

"I know, I know, it's a cat!" yelled a little boy.

"Very good, Eddie. Now, who knows what this animal is called?"

"That's a dog!" piped up the same little boy.

"Right again. And what about this animal?" she asked, holding up a picture of a deer.

Silence fell over the class. After a minute or two, the teacher said, "I'll give you a hint, children. It's something your mother calls your father around the house."

"I know, I know," screamed Eddie. "It's a horny bastard!"

•

What did one goose say to the other goose?

"Ooooh! I've just been peopled!"

•

There was once a Texan who had an unreasonable dislike of elephants. Realizing it bordered on a phobia, he consulted a psychiatrist, who told him it was a fairly common problem. "The cure is straightforward," said the shrink. "You have to go to Africa and shoot one."

The idea appealed to the Texan, so he flew to Kenya and hired a guide to take him on an elephant-hunting safari. The hunter's right-hand man turned out to be a native who in turn hired a bunch of his fellow tribesmen to spread out in a long line, beat drums and blow horns, and drive the elephants toward the blind where the hunters were waiting. As they waited, the noise grew louder and louder until out of the bush with much clanging and shouting burst the head beater. The Texan drew a bead and shot him right between the eyes.

"What the hell'd you do that for?" bellowed the guide. "He's my best beater—I've worked with him for twenty years!"

"If there's anything I hate worse than elephants," drawled the Texan, "it's big, noisy niggers."

•

What do queer deer do?
　Buck-fuck.

•

How can you tell when you've passed an elephant?
　The toilet gets clogged.

•

As a merchant in the caravan business, Ahmed was well aware that a neutered camel can go longer and farther without water than one that hasn't been neutered. But even though he knew he was losing money, he couldn't bear the thought of inflicting such pain on his lead camel, which was really more of a pet than a beast of burden.

Walking through the bazaar one day, he came across the solution to his dilemma: a sign that read "Camels Gelded Without Pain." Making inquiries of the stall's proprietor, he was assured that the operation was quick and absolutely painless. There would be no suffering. A price was negotiated, and the merchant returned the next day with his favorite camel in tow. The camel gelder picked up two bricks, approached the camel from the rear, took aim, and smashed the bricks together with a sound like a thunderclap. Loosing a bellow of agony, the camel collapsed to its knees.

The merchant was horrified. "You promised it would be painless!" he cried, cradling his camel's head.

"Why, it is," explained the gelder, "as long as you don't get your thumbs caught between the bricks."

•

Hearing a noise behind him, a street-corner violinist turned around to see two dogs screwing in the alley. "Don't just stand there," growled one of them, "play 'Bolero.'"

•

Save the whales, eagles, and dolphins—
If you save enough, you can trade them in for lawn furniture!

•

Define BLIND SPOT.
What Dick and Jane do to be cruel.

•

LEPER

What's the opposite of a body builder?
  A leper.

What do you get when you screw a leper?
  A piece of ass.

Why can't lepers give oral sex?
  They lose their heads over it.

Did you hear about the new social program in the leper colony?
  It's called Government Handouts.

Why did the Polish leper go to the ammunition depot?
  To see if he could buy some arms.

•

What's the worst thing about being an epileptic leper?
  Every time you have a seizure, you fall apart.

•

What happened when the leper went to Las Vegas?
  He lost an arm and a leg.

•

Hear the new leper theme songs?
  "Put Your Head on My Shoulder" and "I Want to Hold Your Hand."

•

Did you hear about the leper colony against nuclear proliferation?
  They're already disarmed.

•

How did the leper castrate himself?
  He jerked off.

•

Why was the leper quarterback taken out of the game?
  The last play was a handoff.

•

How come the leper couldn't speak?
  The cat got his tongue.

•

Hear about the new scratch-'n'-sniff stickers for lepers?
  They include a nose.

•

Why was the leper kicked off the relay team?
  He lost the last leg.

•

How come no one in the leper colony could walk after the war?
  They were defeated.

OLD AGE

How do you find an old man in the dark?
  It ain't hard.

•

An old man was dying, and his two sons were at his bedside.
  "Dad, do you have any final requests?" the sons asked.
  "Just one," whispered the old man. "Have my body cremated, and put the ashes in a douche bag. I want to run through there one more time."

•

Three old ladies were sitting on a park bench when a flasher walked up to them and exposed himself. The first old lady had a stroke, and the second old lady had a stroke, but the third old lady's arms were too short to reach.

•

What's the difference between a holdup and a stickup?
  Age.

•

An old man went to bed one night and put his glass eye in a cup. In the middle of the night, he drank the water and inadvertently swallowed the glass eye. Waking up and realizing what he had done, he tottered over to the doctor's office and asked the doctor to retrieve it. Probing every orifice of the old codger's body, the doctor finally located the elusive glass eye in the man's rectum.
  "Do you see it yet, Doc?" the old man asked.
  "No," replied the doctor.
  "That's funny, because I can see you real well!" he hooted.

•

What's the funniest thing you can do at an old people's home?
  Wax the steps and scream, "FIRE."

•

What's invisible and smells like Alpo?
  Old people's farts.

•

A very young woman married a very old man, and on their wedding night she jumped into bed, eager to lose her virginity. The old man held up five fingers.
  "Oh!" the girl giggled. "Does that mean five times?"
  "No," answered the husband. "You get to choose one."

•

How can you tell when a prostitute is over the hill?
 When she asks, "Is it out yet?"

•

"Doctor," an old man complained, "I can't pee."
 "Hmmm," contemplated the doctor. "How old are you?"
 "Eighty-seven," the old man replied.
 "Well, haven't you peed enough?"

•

What do a battery and an old man's dick have in common?
 They both have dry cells.

•

A sweet little old lady and a nice old gent met at a social at the nursing home and decided to tie the knot. After the ceremony, they headed across the street to a motel for their wedding night. "I'll be right back, honey," said the bride, going into the bathroom. When she emerged in her flannel nightie, her groom tottered past her, promising to take just a minute. When he came out in his red PJs, he was greeted by the sight of his new wife standing on her head in the middle of the bed.

"I thought if you couldn't get it up, dearest," she explained sweetly, "you could dunk it in."

MISCELLANEOUS

What's the definition of an anchovy?
A small fish that smells like a finger.

•

A cowboy traveling across the desert came across a lovely woman, naked and battered, her limbs tied to four stakes in the ground.

"Thank God you've come!" she cried. "I was on my way to San Francisco when a whole tribe of Indians attacked our wagon train. They stole our food, kidnapped our children, torched our wagons . . . and raped me over and over."

"Lady," said the cowboy as he unbuckled his belt, "today just ain't your day."

•

What do you get when you drop a piano down a mine shaft?
A-flat miner.

•

How much calcium is in a French kiss?
  Enough to make a bone six inches long.

•

What comes after position 69?
  Mouthwash.

•

What has two balls and eats ants?
  Uncles.

•

Two hillbillies, father and son, live out in the woods. One day the father notices his son looking at underwear ads in the catalog in the outhouse. Sitting him down, he tells Clem it's time for him to go to town and learn about women. "Just go to this here door I'm telling you about, and the gals'll take care of ya," he says.

Soon enough Clem returns from town, walking kind of funny, and Paw can't wait to hear all about it. "Didja go to that door like I tole ya?" he asks.

"I shore did!"

"Did them gals take ya inside and lay ya on a bed?"

"They shore did!"

"Did they take yore clothes off and play with it to get it hard?"

"They shore did!"

"Did they put whipped cream on it?"

"They shore did!"

"Then did they put chocolate sprinkles on it?"

"They shore did!"

"Then did they put a cherry on top of it?"

"They shore did!"

"Then did they eat it?"

"Nope, looked so good I et it myself!"

•

Why are guys so smart and girls so talkative?
  Because guys have two heads and girls have four lips.

•

What's the definition of alimony?
  The screwing you get for the screwing you got.

•

A horny young couple was touring New England, and when they visited a historic cemetery, they couldn't resist screwing vigorously on the long, flat tombstones. The next day, though, the girl visited a local doctor, complaining of a backache.

  After asking her to disrobe and examining her thoroughly, the doctor couldn't find anything wrong. "But by the way," he asked, "how old are you?"

  "Twenty-four," she replied. "Why?"

  The doctor said, "Well, it says on your ass you died in 1787."

•

What do you call someone with a gonorrhea fetish?
  A claptomaniac.

•

Bumper sticker: "98% of all constipated people don't give a shit."

•

A guy runs into a bar and asks for a shot of whiskey and a bottle to go. Doing the shot, he heads out with the bottle, only to return not too much later to repeat his request, barely able to walk. He totters out with another bottle and can hardly see by the time he lurches in to ask for another shot and bottle. The bartender tells him he's too drunk to be served any more.

"You think I'm drunk?" roars the guy. "You think *I'm* drunk? I got a gal out in the car that has a nylon stocking on each arm and every time I kiss her she goes"—makes a farting sound.

•

What do you get when you cross a Xerox copier and a Wurlitzer?

Reproductive organs.

•

Why is sex like pot?

The quality depends on the pusher.

•

What's 72?

Sixty-nine and three voyeurs.

•

Little Mortie got a real surprise when he barged into his parents' room one night. "And you slap me for sucking my *thumb!*" he screamed.

•

A young country girl came to town for a day. She was window shopping when a beautiful pair of red shoes caught her eye, and as she stood admiring them, the clerk came out and asked if he could help her. The girl admitted that she'd spent all her money but that she'd do anything to get her hands on those red shoes.

The clerk thought it over for a moment. "I think we can work out a deal," he told her. "Go lie down on the couch in the back room." Soon he came in and closed the door. "So do you want those shoes bad enough to put out for them?" he asked. When she nodded, he pulled down his pants, exposing a hard-on about nine inches long. "Honey, I'll screw you with this big cock of mine until you squirm with pleasure and scream in ecstasy and go wild with desire."

"I don't get much of a kick out of sex, but go right ahead," said the girl, spreading her legs and lying back. Sure she couldn't last long, the salesman started pumping away, but she lay there like a dishrag. Pretty soon he'd come twice and began to worry about getting soft, so he started going at it for all he was worth. Sure enough he felt her arms go around his neck and her legs tighten around his waist. "Best fuck you've ever had, right?" chortled the man. "In a couple of seconds you'll be coming like crazy."

"Oh, no, it's not that," said the girl. "I'm just trying on my new shoes."

•

Definition of a baby pacifier?
A bust in the mouth.

•

Definition of a papoose?
A consolation prize for taking a chance on an Indian blanket.

•

Definition of a parlor game?
You and the maid are alone in the parlor, and she's game.

•

A wealthy king is sailing the seven seas with his harem, court, and jester, when a typhoon comes up and the ship goes down. Everyone is drowned except the king and the jester, who manage to paddle to a desert island. The king is stranded, deprived of his yacht, his wealth, and his harem. Well, after a week, he was at his wit's end. . . .

•

What do you call a reporter's sperm?
Journaljism.

•

Gus went to see a lawyer about a divorce. "What grounds do you have?" the lawyer asked.

"The usual: front yard, back yard, and a tiny little strip on each side," Gus elaborated.

"I meant, do you have a grudge?" the attorney explained.

"Yeah, we have one, but we keep it so full of trash, we can't get the car in it."

"Let me be more specific. Is your wife a nagger?" the lawyer sighed.

"No," said Gus, "but I caught her screwing one, and that's why I want the divorce."

•

A black woman with eight children happened to run across a childhood friend of hers on the street corner. "Myrna," she asked, "how come you got no kids?"

"I practice preventive measures," was the answer.

"Preventive measures? What's that?" asked Evelyn.

"I use two saucers and a box. I'm a lot taller than my husband, and we like to screw standing up. When he gets a hard-on, I pull up my dress, spread my legs, and put the two saucers on the table. He stands up on the box so he can get all the way inside me and starts jumping up and down."

"So where does all this get you?" asked Evelyn, confused.

"That's when I got to watch him very closely. When his eyes get big as those two saucers, I kick the box out from under him."

•

A girl walked into the corner hardware store, found the hinges she was looking for, and brought them up to the counter.

"Need a screw for those hinges?" asked the proprietor.

"No," she answered after reflecting for a bit, "but how about a blow job for the toaster in the back?"

•

Heard about the new funeral parlor in Malibu?
  It's called "Death 'N' Things."

•

Favorite bumper stickers:
  I Try to Run Over Small Animals
  Honk If You Have Herpes
  Beam Me Up, Scotty—This Planet Sucks
  All Extremists Should Be Killed

•

What's white and squirms up skirts?
  Uncle Ben's Perverted Rice.

•

Moe and Joe were driving and drinking beer, and pretty soon Moe had to take a leak. He asked Joe to pull over, walked into a field, and started to pee. Suddenly Mother Nature materialized in front of him and said sternly, "I've caught you pissing on my buttercups. As punishment, from now on when you eat anything with butter in it, you'll get sick as a dog."

Rather shaken, Moe walked back to the car and told his friend what had happened.

"Cheer up," said Joe. "You could've been pissing on the pussy willows."

•

What do hot bodies get on cold nights?
  Sniffylis.

·

A handsome fellow was traveling across the country and was out in the middle of the Iowa cornfields when night started to fall. Coming up to a farmhouse, he asked the farmer if he could put him up for the night. The farmer explained that he didn't want the guy sleeping under the same roof as his lovely daughter, but gave him permission to sleep in the barn. As the traveler headed for the barn, the farmer shouted after him that he was putting a barricade of eggs around his daughter's room just in case he should get any ideas. "If a single egg's broken in the morning," he yelled, "I'll shoot you in the back."

The fellow bedded down comfortably enough in the hay, but all night he was tossing and turning, thinking of the farmer's daughter. Finally he couldn't take it anymore. He ran inside, through the wall of eggs and into the girl's room, where she showed him a very good time till it was almost dawn. Then, in something of a panic, he left the room and began frantically gluing all the eggs back together.

The last one had just been set in place when the farmer came out of his room. "Boy, have you got willpower," he commented, looking admiringly at his guest. "Not a single egg broken. Just for that, you get breakfast on the house." Taking five eggs off the pile, the farmer took them into the kitchen and cracked the first one against the edge of a bowl. Nothing came out. He cracked the second egg and still nothing came out. And the third, fourth, and fifth, and of course they were all empty. "Goddamn rooster's been using a rubber again!" groaned the farmer.

·

Boy: "Let's play Carnival."
Girl: "How?"
Boy: "You sit on my face and I try to guess your weight."

·

How many USC football players does it take to change a light bulb?

Just one, but he got an A for it.

•

Instructions for love:

Remove wrapper from all body parts and place on large, flat surface.

Place Part A against Part B.

Locate Joint C and insert into Slot D.

Slide Joint C in carefully to insure proper fit.

Tighten nuts.

•

What goes, "Huff, thud, huff, thud, huff, squish?"

A jogger stepping in dog shit.

•

A fellow walked into a nice-looking bar, sat down, and ordered a drink. As he sat there, he noticed people walking in and out of a back room, but he didn't really think twice about it. Ordering another drink, he asked the bartender casually, "So what do people around here do for excitement?"

"See that number on the back of your seat?" answered the bartender. "If your number's called, you get a free piece of ass."

"Wow, that sounds great," said the guy, deciding to stick around. When it came time to order another drink, he turned to the guy next to him and griped, "Hell, I've been here over an hour—how do you win at this thing?"

The man gave him a conspiratorial wink and said, "Don't give up, buddy. Hell, my wife has already won five times!"

•

What's this? (Curl both sides of your tongue.)
  Blower's cramp.

•

Why did the chicken cross the road? It wanted to get to the other side. Why did the dead baby cross the road? It was stapled to the chicken. Why did the cannibal cross? It was trying to eat the dead baby stapled to the chicken that was desperately trying to get to the other side. Why did the punk cross the road? To kick the cannibal trying to eat the dead baby that was stapled to the chicken trying to get to the other side. Why did the policeman cross the road? To arrest the punk trying to kick the cannibal eating the dead baby that was stapled to the chicken. Why did the Polack cross the road? To ask the policeman who was trying to arrest the punker who was kicking the cannibal who was eating the dead baby which was stapled to the chicken how to get back across. Why did the hooker cross the road? To fuck the Polack who was trying to ask the policemen who was arresting the punk who was kicking the cannibal who was eating the dead baby stapled to the chicken how to get back across. Why did the milkman cross the road? He didn't. He was sick of this joke.

•

Why do women have a speed limit of sixty-eight?
  When they hit sixty-nine, they blow a rod.

•

Where does the Ku Klux Klan buy its costumes?
  At the K-K-K Mart.

•

How many New Yorkers does it take to screw in a light bulb?
  None of your fuckin' business.

•

A ship was wrecked in a storm, leaving the captain and seven of his crew adrift in a lifeboat. After two weeks at sea, supplies were running low and the captain decided that instead of having them all starve to death, he would shoot himself and let the men eat his body. As he put the loaded revolver to his temple, the young second mate begged, "Oh, Captain, Captain, don't shoot yourself in the head."

"I have to do what I have to do, my boy," the captain explained gently.

"But you don't understand, sir," said the sailor. "Brains are my favorite dish."

•

What do video games and *Playboy* have in common?
    They both improve hand-eye coordination.

•

Why is a boss like a diaper?
    He's always on your ass and usually full of shit.

•

What's the difference between a school bus and a cucumber?
    All the little pricks are on the outside of a cucumber.

•

One day a farmer went out to the barn to feed his cow. As he was pouring the food into the cow's trough, the cow kicked it over, spilling feed everywhere.

"That's one," said the farmer.

The next day the cow knocked down a fence the farmer had spent two weeks repairing.

"That's two," warned the farmer.

The following morning, while the farmer was milking the cow, it knocked the bucket over, spilling milk all over the ground.

"That's three," said the farmer, and he got his shotgun and shot the cow through the head.

His wife heard the gun blast and ran out to the barn. "Why the hell did you kill the cow?" she yelled when she saw the dead cow and her husband with a smoking shotgun in his hands.

"That's one," he said.

•

Why are hotdogs America's national food?
Because they taste better than dildos.

•

Sign at a funeral parlor: "Our staff will stuff your stiff."
Sign at the whorehouse next door: "Our stuff will stiff your staff."

•

What's the new venereal disease that only affects foot fetishists?
Athlete's tongue.

•

What did one bulldozer say to the other?
"Did the earth move for you too?"

•

"You just have minor cuts on your buttocks," the doctor reported. "What happened?"

"Well, you see," the patient explained, "I was screwing my girlfriend when all of a sudden the chandelier fell."

"Wow!" exclaimed the doctor. "You're a very lucky man."

"You're telling me," the patient said with a sigh of relief. "A minute sooner and I would have had a fractured skull!"

TOO TASTELESS
TO BE INCLUDED

What's the difference between Baby Fae's death and the death of a baboon?

The baboon's death wasn't funny.

•

One day Daphne decided to invite her boyfriend over even though her dad was in the living room reading the paper. She and Mike crept up the stairs without being seen, but in a little while her father heard strange noises coming from the bedroom: thumps, squeaks, and moans, among other things. Going to the foot of the stairs, he shouted, "Daphne, you get down here! What's all that noise?"

In a few minutes a breathless Daphne and a red-faced Mike ran down the stairs. "What the hell were you two doing up there?" bellowed Daphne's father.

Daphne thought for minute and said, "We were making sandwiches, Dad."

"Oh, sure," he retorted, "and I suppose that's mayonnaise running down your leg?"

•

How do you make Instant Easter?
Two boards and a Jew.

•

Why do Dobermans lick their asses?
To get the taste of black people out of their mouths.

•

Why can't Jews eat Germans?
Because they give them gas.

•

Bored with the thought of another night barhopping and picking up some chicks, John came up with the idea of propositioning a really old broad. It'd be a change of pace, and might even be good for some laughs with the guys after the fact. So he went to his favorite bar, and after about an hour a woman who looked to be about ninety years old came in. John went over, sat down next to her, and after a couple of minutes came right to the point: would she be interested in coming over to his place for some action?

The old bird jumped at the chance, and no sooner had they walked into his place than she dragged him into the bedroom, ripped off her clothes, and jumped on top of him. He was a little taken aback but decided to make the best of it, kissing her lips, then her wrinkly neck, then her cleavage and her saggy tits. Next he sucked a bit on one of her withered nipples, and much to his amazement out came some warm liquid. "Man, that's some good-tasting juice," he said, looking up in surprise. "But aren't you kind of old to be giving milk?"

"Yes, I am, sonny," cackled the old broad, "but I'm not too old to have cancer!"

•

What's the first thing you do when you see somebody choking?
  Laugh.
What's the second thing you do?
  Offer them more food.

·

What's a Polish abortion?
  A hungry rat on a string.

·

What looks like a walrus and sees stars?
  A seal being clubbed.

·

A woman was sitting on the sofa breast-feeding her child when all of a sudden she got her period. The baby stuck his head up and said, "Aw, Ma, I coulda had a V-Eight."

·

What's the definition of a pizza?
  An abortion on toast.

·

What's grosser than gross?
  When Siamese twins are attached at the mouth and one throws up.

·

This little boy about ten years old walks into a whorehouse dragging a dead frog on a string behind him. Walking up to the madam, he says, "I would like a girl for the evening."
  "I'm sorry, but I can't help you. You're too young," says the madam.

The little boy takes two hundred dollars out of his wallet and hands it over. "One lady, coming right up," she says.

"One condition," says the little boy. "The lady has to have active herpes."

"I'm sorry, but I can't help you. All my girls are clean," says the madam.

The little boy takes another two hundred dollars out of his wallet, and she says, "One dirty lady, coming right up." So the little boy goes upstairs with the prostitute. About twenty-five minutes later the boy comes downstairs all happy and smiling, still dragging his dead frog behind him. As he heads out the door, the madam says, "May I ask you a question? Why did you insist on a woman with herpes?"

"It goes like this," says the little boy. "When I get home tonight, my babysitter will be there. I'll make love with her, and she'll get the herpes. When my parents get back, my dad will drive the babysitter home, screw the babysitter, and catch the herpes. When he comes in, he'll make love with my mom, and she'll catch it. Tomorrow morning about eight my father will leave for work. At about ten the milkman gets there, and he's the bastard who killed my FROG."

•

What makes thousands of dollars and still begs?
   Blanche Knott.

*Ray Charles

Would you like to see your favorite tasteless joke(s) in print? If so, send them to:

Blanche Knott
% St. Martin's Press
175 Fifth Avenue
New York, New York 10010

Remember, no compensation or credit can be given, and only those tasteless enough will be included!

What do you call a series of books that will have you groaning with laughter?

Blanche Knott's Truly Tasteless Jokes

Over 3 million copies of Truly Tasteless Jokes in print!

TRULY TASTELESS JOKES IV
_____90365-0 $2.95 U.S.   _____90366-9 $3.50 Can.

TRULY TASTELESS JOKES V
_____90371-5 $2.95 U.S.   _____90372-3 $3.50 Can.

and coming soon

TRULY TASTELESS JOKES VI
_____90361-8 $2.95 U.S.   _____90373-1 $3.75 Can.

THE TRULY TASTELESS JOKE-A-DATE BOOK 1987
_____90485-1 $3.95 U.S.   _____90523-8 $4.95 Can.

Spiral bound for easy access to a laugh a day!

Exercise Your Mind
with Puzzles, Games, and Brain Teasers

DR. CRYPTON'S MIND BENDERS
A brilliant barrage of zany intellectual games from the man
Chicago magazine called, "the smartest man in the world."
_____ 90182-8 $3.95 U.S.   _____ 90183-6 $4.95 Can.

THE LITTLE MAZE BOOK by the Diagram Group
Seventy unique mazes to dazzle the eye while they engage the
mind.
_____ 90239-5 $3.50 U.S.

THE SUNDAY TIMES BOOK OF BRAIN TEASERS,
compiled and edited by Victor Bryant and Ronald Postil
Fifty hard (very hard!) master problems—the ultimate chal-
lenge for truly serious competitors.
_____ 90338-3 $3.95 U.S.

and coming soon

THE CROSSWORDER'S LIST BOOK by John E. Brown
and Margaret Brown
Over 30,000 words arranged by subject—you'll never be
stumped for a three letter word for SEA BIRD again!
_____ 90092-9 $3.50 U.S.   _____ 90574-2 $4.50 Can.

NOW AVAILABLE AT YOUR BOOKSTORE!

The Hottest...
from St. Martin's Press!